In Search of the Unusual in Ryedale and the North York Moors

by
Eileen Rennison

HUTTON PRESS
1993

Published by
The Hutton Press Ltd.,
130 Canada Drive, Cherry Burton, Beverley
East Yorkshire HU17 7SB

Copyright © 1993

Printed and bound by

Clifford Ward & Co. (Bridlington) Ltd.,
55 West Street, Bridlington, East Yorkshire,
YO15 3DZ

ISBN 1 872167 53 5

CONTENTS

Page

Acknowledgements. 4

Introduction. 5

1. Amotherby. Stone Effigy in St. Helen's Church. 7
2. Appleton-le-Moors, Three Faces. 8
3. Beckhole. Birch Hall Inn Sign. 9
4. Bilsdale. The Cross at a Pub. 10
5. Bossall. Harvard Connection. 11
6. Brompton-by-Sawdon. A Poet's Marriage Certificate. 12
7. Buttercrambe. The Church Angle. 13
8. Castle Howard. Bulmer Beacon. 14
9. Cawton. A Reminder of the Past. 15
10. Clifton Moor. Weathervane. 16
11. Coxwold. Secret Painting at Shandy Hall. 17
    Two Stones and a Question of Dates. 17
    The Altar Rail, Coxwold Church. 17
12. Cropton. The New Inn. 19
13. Dalby. Turf Maze. 20
14. Ebberston. The Smallest Stately Home. 21
15. Egton Bridge. The Mass House. 22
16. Flaxton. Grazing Rights. 23
17. Foston. A Famous Rector. 24
18. Fylingthorpe. A Temple for Pigs. 25
19. Gillamoor. Four faces. 26
20. Glaisdale. Beggar's Bridge. 27
21. Goathland. Wade's Causeway, Wheeldale Moor. 28
    An Anchor in the Churchyard. 28
22. Great Ayton. Cook's Family Gravestone. 29
23. Helmsley. Greek Temples and a Record Tree. 30
24. Helmsley Bank. Controversial Sculpture. 31
25. Hinderwell. St. Hilda's Well. 32

Page

26. The Hole of Horcum. 33
27. Hovingham. Hovingham Hall. 34
    Hovingham School. 34
28. Hutton-le-Hole. Witch Posts. 35
29. Kilburn. The White Horse. 36
30. Kirkdale. Saxon Sundial, St. Gregory's Minster. 38
31. Lastingham. The Shrine of St. Cedd. 39
32. Littlebeck. The Hermitage. 40
33. Moorland Crosses. Ralph Cross. 41
    (Young Ralph and Old Ralph). 41
    Lilla Cross. 41
    Fat Betty. 41
34. Nawton. An Unusual Bus Shelter. 43
35. Nether Silton. A Mysterious Inscription. 44
36. Oldstead. Mount Snever Observatory. 45
37. Osmotherley. Chequers Inn. 46
    Mount Grace Priory. A very early serving-hatch. 46
    Outdoor Table and Pulpit. 46
38. Pickering. American Associations. 48
39. Port Mulgrave. The Hidden Harbour. 49
40. Saltersgate. The Turf Fire that Never Goes Out. 50
41. Scotch Corner. Lonely Chapel of Remembrance. 51
42. Sheriff Hutton. The Tomb of the Young Prince. 52
43. Sinnington. A Bridge over Nothing. 53
44. Staithes. The Traditional Bonnet. 54
45. Stonegrave. Wills in Stone. 55
46. Westerdale. Bulmer's Stone. 56
47. Wharram Percy. The Lost Village. 58
48. Whitby. The Hand of Glory. 59
    The Whalebone Monument. 60

ACKNOWLEDGEMENTS

Some of the items in this book have been extracted from articles by the author which have been previously published in the *Dalesman Magazine* and *The Lady*.

The following books have been consulted in compiling this book:-

The Priest of the Moors, by Elizabeth Hamilton, pub. 1980 by Darton, Longman & Todd. London.
Yorkshire. by G. Bernard Wood, pub. 1967 by Batsford, London.
Inside the North York Moors, by Harry Mead, pub. 1978 by David & Charles, London.
Round and About the North Yorkshire Moors, by Tom Scott Burns, pub. 1987 by M. T. D. Rigg Publications, Guiseley.
Murders and Mysteries from the North York Moors, by Peter N. Walker, pub. 1988 by Robert Hale, London.
Beastly Buildings, by Lucinda Lambton, pub. 1985 by Jonathan Cape, London.

The author acknowledges the courtesy of the Whitby Literary and Philosophical Society in granting permission to publish the photograph of the Hand of Glory in Whitby Museum, and the Ryedale Folk Museum for the use of the photograph of the Witch Post.

Thanks are also due to all those persons whose properties are pictured and featured, making this book possible.

INTRODUCTION

Ryedale and the North York Moors abound in beautiful places and magnificent scenery which are loved and admired by residents and visitors alike, and have been the subject of many interesting books. This book aims to show, not the beauty of the area, but some of its wealth of fascinating curiosities and oddities. Unusual buildings and other objects of interest: the tomb of the young prince, son of Richard III at Sheriff Hutton; the great Saxon sundial at St. Gregory's Minster; the inn sign painted by a Royal Academician at Beckhole; monuments, inscriptions, follies; some well known, some less so but all unusual and worthwhile seeing; some deserving of a special journey to see them and others not to be missed if one is in the vicinity.

The book makes no claim to being a comprehensive review of all the unusual places of interest in the area. There are doubtless many more. These are simply the ones which are known to me and which I have seen for myself. Though I have defined my area of investigation as Ryedale and the North York Moors it will soon become apparent to the reader that I have not confined myself to the valley of the River Rye. The Ryedale in question is in fact the administrative area of Ryedale District Council, which stretches from the very edge of the city of York in the south to the highest parts of the North York Moors in the north and across from the Wolds in the east to the Howardian Hills to the west. Similarly I have allowed myself some leeway in straying occasionally beyond the borders of the North York Moors National Park, to include for example Whitby, which though not within the National Park is nevertheless inseparable to Yorkshire men and women from the North York Moors.

I have felt justified in including Wordsworth's marriage certificate at Brompton church though the village falls just outside both Ryedale District and the National Park, because of his many connections with other places within both areas.

It is hoped that the reader will forgive any such small trespasses, and that the items within these pages will interest, surprise or amuse, and persuade him or her to add to his or her pleasure and knowledge in exploring the area.

The places of interest are arranged simply in alphabetical order and information is provided to help in locating them.

Eileen Rennison
York.
May 1993

1. AMOTHERBY

Stone Effigy in St. Helen's Church

Amotherby lies at right angles to the B1257 road from Malton to Helmsley approximately 3 miles from Malton.

In the Sanctuary of St. Helen's Church at Amotherby is the stone effigy of a knight, Sir John de Bordeston. Sir John, who died in 1329, seems to have been a belligerent and turbulent character, constantly involved in lengthy disputes over grazing rights with the Prior of Old Malton, leading to fighting between his and the Prior's men, and even to his being excommunicated from the Church for a time in 1303.

He wears a hood of chainmail with a filet or band around his brow, and carries a shield with his coat of arms of three boars' heads; his legs are crossed, his feet rest on a lion and his hands are clasped in prayer. He may seem at first glance much like many other effigies to be found in churches throughout the country. Even his disputatious character does not distinguish him from many other knights at that time. However his effigy is in fact a rare and singular one in that it is one of only seven known examples of a knight shown wearing a surcoat with sleeves. The more usual surcoat is a sleeveless garment worn over armour as part of the insignia of knighthood.

At the opposite end of the church, beside the South Door is a modern stained glass window. With its simple design of a man with a wheelbarrow it is a memorial to a more humble but worthy parishioner; a touching and eloquent tribute by his friends and admirers to Alan Hornby, a mentally retarded man who devoted himself to the care and maintenance of the churchyard until his death in 1968.

(a) Photograph by Eileen Rennison
(b) Photograph by Richard Hebblethwaite

2. APPLETON-LE-MOORS

Three Faces

Appleton-le-Moors is situated about 1¾ miles off the A170 Pickering to Helmsley road, taking a right turn some 5½ miles from Pickering.

The stone cottages in the attractively named village of Appleton-le-Moors are typical of those found almost anywhere on the North York Moors, but an extra and amusing feature is to be seen on one small cottage next to the Post Office in the main street. The name of the cottage is *Three Faces*, and the reason is plain to see, for carved into a stone above an inscription — indecipherable to me — over the door are the three faces in question.

Said to be a satirical portrayal of the Lawyer, the Doctor and the Clergyman, there is nothing to indicate which is which and one must put one's own interpretation on them. The face on the left, thin with furrowed brow, short wig and thin-lipped, tightly closed mouth, seems to me to fit the stereotype of the dry-as-dust clever lawyer. In the centre the full face with the long hair or wig, the well fed look yet with the mouth turned down as if the bearer of bad news or perhaps in disgust of mankind, I take to be the doctor. On the right the thin face with wild hair and fanatical eyes, the mouth open as if preaching hell-fire, must surely represent the clergyman. Or have I got it all wrong? See for yourself and decide.

Three Faces
Photographs by Richard Hebblethwaite.

3. BECKHOLE

Birch Hall Inn sign

Beckhole is a mile beyond Goathland which lies 3 miles off the A169 Pickering to Whitby road, taking a left turn about 11 miles out of Pickering, within sight of the Fyling-dales Early Warning station. Goathland village is provided with a public Car Park and Beckhole is signposted from the centre of the village.

Beckhole is a tiny attractive hamlet nestling in a fold of the Moors, approachable on foot or by car, by the green pathway of a disused railway track or by road, from Goathland a mile away. By road a steep z-bend takes one suddenly into view of the tiny hidden cluster of houses beyond a bridge crossing the beck at the foot of the hill. There, just beside the bridge is the little whitewashed *Birch Hall Inn* with the rather unusual sight of a picture hanging on the wall, on the outside of the house. Framed and under glass, the scene depicted is the view from the bridge along the beck as it runs through the steep wooded gorge behind the inn.

It was painted by the artist Algernon Newton R.A. as a token of his affection for Beckhole, where he had a house and studio during the Second World War. He painted his picture originally on a material that weathered badly and so he painted a second, the present version, on metal protected by glass. If the author's memory can be relied on the original was on a larger scale than the present picture. But after so many years the memory can play tricks on one.

Algernon Newton was the father of the noted actor Robert Newton, well remembered for his portrayal of Long John Silver in Treasure Island. He was born in 1880 and died in 1968 and painted many townscapes of his native London. In 1940 he bought his house and studio in Beckhole and turned to landscapes of the locality. He was made a Royal Academician in 1943 but was an established and successful artist before coming to Beckhole and had been one of the artists chosen to produce art works for the great liner *Queen Mary* when she was built. His pictures are to be found in public galleries throughout the country, but none surely so publicly displayed as the one on the inn by the roadside at Beckhole?

Birch Hall Inn sign.
Photograph by Richard Hebblethwaite.

4. BILSDALE

The cross at a pub

'Spout House' and the 'Sun Inn' are at the roadside on the B1257 Helmsley to Stokesley road at Chop Gate, approximately 12 miles from Helmsley. Urra lies 2 miles off to the right about 1 mile further along the road.

Spout House, one of the oldest buildings in the National Park, is an interesting, long, low, thatched house of cruck construction dating from 1550. Named from a spring in the hillside behind it, it was first licensed as an inn in 1714 and renamed the *Sun Inn*, but the old name still stuck.

Today it is possible for the visitor to see its traditionally furnished interior, any day except Thursday, from Easter to October between 10 am and 4 pm. An unusual reminder of a former sporting patron can be seen anytime outside the new *Sun Inn* close by.

In 1902, Bobby Dowson who was wicket-keeper for *Spout House* cricket club, and who served as whipper for the ancient Bilsdale Hunt for over sixty years, died. At his funeral horse and hounds accompanied his coffin and his hunting clothes were buried in the grave with him, but his headstone which was carved with a fox's head and his hunting whips was regarded for that reason, by the vicar, as unsuitable for inclusion in consecrated ground.

For twelve years it lay outside the churchyard gate, until, when the new *Sun Inn* was being built across the yard from the old *Spout House*, Bobby's sporting friends decided that since he had been very fond of the old pub and popular there, the new inn would be an appropriate site for his memorial. And so the cross with its fox's head and whips was placed by the entrance to the *Sun Inn* beside *Spout House*, where it still stands, while in the churchyard at Urra a small plain cross commemorates Bobby Dowson and declares simply that:

No finer sportsman ever followed hounds
O'er moors and fields he knew for thirty miles around.

The cross at a Pub – Photographs by Eileen Rennison

5. BOSSALL

Harvard connection

Bossall lies off the A64 between Malton and York. Some 10½ miles from Malton take the turn off to Claxton. Bossall is beyond Claxton about 2½ miles from the main road.

Bossall was once a large and important village, a centre of religious importance with an imposing church founded by Archbishop Boss. Today the village consists of only a few houses, having been all but destroyed by the Black Death, and never subsequently recovered from the devastation.

St. Botolph's church at Bossall, with its square central tower and Norman arched doorway, is well worth a visit in its own right, but it also contains something which gives it an interesting connection with Harvard University in Amerca. It was here that the Rev. Thomas Shepard, one of the founders of that institution, was married to a Miss Margaret Tutville in 1632. A copy of the church records registering the fact is displayed in the church.

Harvard, the senior university of the United States of America, developed from a college founded in 1636 by some Cambridge graduates, the Rev. Shepard amongst them, in the hamlet of New Towne just outside Boston, Massachusetts. They named it Cambridge after their own seat of learning, but in 1638 when the Rev. John Harvard, citizen of Charlestown but a native of Southwark, London, and also a Cambridge man, died leaving all his books and half his estate to the college, it took the name of its benefactor to become Harvard College. It later achieved university status and grew, broadening its fields of study from its original somewhat narrow sectarian lines to its present wide-ranging importance.

A further claim which Bossall can make to the unusual lies is the fact that in 1988 the churchyard was designated a Site of Special Scientific Interest because of the number and variety of wild flowers to be found within its boundaries. Spring flowers in particular grow there in profusion: snowdrops, primroses, wild daffodils, violets and cowslips being only the most familiar amongst them, but nevertheless ones which are becoming increasingly rare in the fields and hedgerows.

St. Boltoph's church, Bossall
Photograph by Eileen Rennison

6. BROMPTON by SAWDON

A poet's marriage certificate

Brompton by Sawdon is approximately 7 miles from Scarborough and 9 miles from Pickering on the A170 road. Gallow's Hill Farm lies midway between Brompton and Wykeham.

The poet William Wordsworth, poet of the Lake District, married Mary Hutchinson, as he described it, 'under the pretty little spire of Brompton Parish Church'. A copy of their marriage certificate can be seen in the church in the village of Brompton by Sawdon. William and Mary were married very quietly by licence on 4th October 1802 in the presence only of three of Mary's brothers and two sisters. Strangely, William's sister Dorothy did not accompany her beloved brother to the church to see him married to her best friend, but awaited their return to Gallows Hill Farm near Wykeham where Mary lived with a brother. Dorothy can hardly have disapproved of the marriage to Mary who was a childhood friend, so perhaps she had one of the sick headaches to which she was prone, brought on by the excitement and emotion, even possibly some feelings of jealousy at the prospect of sharing both her brother and her friend. Mary's older relatives and guardians certainly did disapprove and cut her off on her marriage to William, whom they regarded as a 'vagabond'. Despite that, their wedding day was the beginning of a long and contented married life, though it has been suggested that William only really fell in love with Mary after some ten years of marriage.

Dorothy Wordsworth described the church at Brompton as 'a sweet church and churchyard' and it is indeed in a lovely setting. Of thirteenth to fifteenth century architecture with a square tower and broach spire, the church stands in an elevated position at the back of Brompton village over-looking a small lake.

The visitor to Brompton church can now find further interest and information about Wordsworth and his links with North Yorkshire by travelling the short distance to Mary Hutchinson's old home, Gallows Hill Farm, where the Wordsworth and Coleridge Gallery has recently been established by retired solicitor Michael Harrison. Both poets were frequent visitors there: Wordsworth because of Mary, and Coleridge, though married, to see Mary's sister Sara with whom he was hopelessly in love.

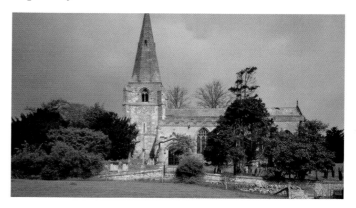

Brompton by Sawdon Church
Photograph by Eileen Rennison

A Poet's Marriage Certificate
Photograph by Richard Hebblethwaite

7. BUTTERCRAMBE

The church angle

Buttercrambe lies off the A64 between Malton and York. Turn off to Claxton about 10½ miles from Malton and Buttercrambe is about 4 miles beyond Claxton.

The church of St. John the Evangelist in the village of Buttercrambe dates originally from 1240 and was a Chapel of Ease to the once more important church at nearby Bossall. It has seen many later alterations and has many features of interest to the visitor.

On entering the door one is faced immediately by one of these; the fact that one must negotiate four steps, not up, but more unusually down, into the Nave. But perhaps the most interesting and unusual feature above all of the church is not at first readily apparent.

Most people are aware that the plan of many churches with Nave, Chancel and Transepts forms a symbol of the Cross. The church at Buttercrambe takes symbolism a step further in that the Chancel is built at a slight angle to the Nave representing Christ's head inclined upon the Cross. The angle is such that it could be overlooked by the unaware. However, by standing in the middle of the centre aisle towards the back of the Nave and looking through the Chancel Arch to the altar, it is possible to see that the window above it appears slightly off-centre of the arch, thus indicating the angling of the Chancel.

It is also possible for the discerning eye to recognise this subtle and interesting architectural symbolism from outside the church, and on raising one's eye to the roof yet another interesting feature can be observed. The church has neither spire nor tower. The bells are housed in a bellcote which is of an uncommon design. The symbol of the cross which can be found as a regular feature of the main body of church buildings everywhere, is here carried into the smaller detail of the bellcote, which is built in the shape of a cross surmounted by a tiny steeple.

The Church Angle
Photograph by Eileen Rennison

8. CASTLE HOWARD

Bulmer Beacon

From the A64 out of Malton towards York turn off right at Barton Hill at the bottom of Whitwell Hill and follow the signs to Castle Howard for about 2 miles. Bulmer Beacon stands beside the road on the left.

Motorists turning off the main road from Malton or York to visit Castle Howard will find themselves on twisting country roads climbing the Howardian Hills. On the edge of the Castle Howard estate, overlooking the farmlands from the hillside, they cannot fail to see and perhaps wonder about the tall blackened column standing in isolation in a fenced enclosure by the roadside.

For a long time a feature of the countryside in these parts and popularly known as Bulmer Beacon — taking the name from the village of Bulmer nearby — it is in fact a monument to the seventh Earl of Carlisle, an ancestor of the Howards of Castle Howard and a prominent politician of his day.

Today the monument consists of the tall central column set on a wide, stepped plinth, with smaller columns topped by heraldic helmets at its four corners, but it was indeed originally a beacon with a metal 'basket' to contain the flames on top of the central column. Whether it was ever lit as a beacon or even intended to be more than decorative and symbolic is doubtful. At one time the metal beacon holder hung sadly and precariously in a state of dilapidation, making it dangerous to approach, until it was finally removed, leaving the monument as it is today.

If one climbs the steps of the plinth it is possible to read the inscriptions which run round the four sides of the square base of the column. On one side are the words '*In memory of George William Frederick*' and on the opposite side '*VIIth Earl of Carlisle, Viscount Morpeth K.C.*' The remaining two sides carry somewhat longer inscriptions. On the one we are told that '*He to whom the monument was raised AD MDCCCLXIX in private life was loved by all who knew him. By his public conduct won the respect of his country and left behind the bright example of a true patriot and earnest Christian*', and on the other, '*He to whom this monument was raised by public subscription during twelve years represented in the House of Commons firstly Yorkshire secondly the West Riding and during eight years was Viceroy of Ireland.*'

It is a pity that this impressive monument has lost its most unusual feature, but even without it, it remains, because of its size and its roadside countryside situation an interesting and arresting sight.

Bulmer Beacon
Photograph by Richard Hebblethwaite

9. CAWTON

A reminder of the Past

At Stonegrave 5½ miles from Helmsley on the B1257 turn right for Gilling. Cawton is about 1½ miles ahead.

Once, not so very long ago, milk churns stood on their little wooden platforms by almost every farmhouse gate, waiting to be collected by the milk lorries going around the countryside. Today, methods of milking, and collection and distribution of milk have all changed and become more sophisticated. Milk churns are no longer a common sight at the roadside.

If you are passing through the little village of Cawton on the road between Stonegrave and Gilling look out for a reminder of this rural practice of the past. Three of these old farming relics have been used to make a jolly and individual house-sign, beside the road outside Spring Farm Cottage.

A reminder of the past – Photograph by Eileen Rennison

10. CLIFTON MOOR

Weathervane

Clifton Moor Shopping and Industrial Complex is beside the A1237 road on the Northern outskirts of York, in the sector of the Ring-road which lies between the A19 to Thirsk and the B1363 to Helmsley.

The traditional form for a weathervane is a cock. Indeed the name of weathercock is often used as a general term. A flying pennant is also traditional and forms of particular relevance to a building or its owners are frequently to be seen, for example, a horse on a riding school, or other figures and objects involved in the activities carried on within the premises. The passer-by therefore on the York bypass just within the borders of Ryedale District, where it skirts the Clifton Moor Shopping Complex, may be surprised to see the weathervane on the Tesco supermarket. What, he or she may wonder, can be its possible connection to the admittedly wide range of goods on sale there? Three areoplanes flying in formation against a background cloud seem to have little to do with modern retailing activities. They are there in fact as a tribute to the airmen and women who were once stationed on the spot during the Second World War, for the Shopping Complex is built on the site of the long disused Clifton Aerodrome and commemorates them in this small unusual detail.

A new pub serving the nearby housing estate is also claimed to honour the personnel who served at Clifton with its name *The Flying Legends*; a name given after much local controversy and complaint when the originally chosen name was felt to have no relevance to the pub's situation and to ignore the area's past history.

A more formal memorial to the men and women who repaired and kept the Halifax bombers in the air at Clifton airfield can be found on the corner of Kettlestring Lane in the Industrial Estate behind the Shopping Complex. A simple column and plaque, it was unveiled by a local Second World War veteran of the Royal Air Force in the presence of dignitaries from Ryedale and the local councils and other interested parties.

Weathervane
Photograph by Richard Hebblethwaite

11. COXWOLD

Take the A170 out of Helmsley to Thirsk. Turn left about 4 miles out following signs to Wass and Coxwold for a further 4 miles approximately. Turn right up the village street. Shandy Hall is at the end of the street on the right beyond the church on the left. The Hall is open to the public June-September, Wed. 2-4.30pm: Sun. 2.30-4,30pm:

Secret Painting at Shandy Hall

Shandy Hall at Coxwold derives its name from the novel Tristram Shandy by Laurence Sterne which he wrote when he was living there as curate. A visit to the house, an attractive and fascinatingly irregular building, of gables, sloping roof, tall chimneys and walls of brick and stone, is a unique experience. Restored to the condition in which Sterne left it in 1767 and filled with items of interest to scholars and casual visitors alike, Shandy Hall is open to the public during the summer months. Its low-ceilinged panelled rooms are a picture of eighteenth century comfort and elegance, but the panelling itself hides a secret of the house's ancient history.

It was originally a medieval open hall dwelling, and one is suddenly faced with the unexpected evidence of its long history as a priest's house when an attendant opens a section of panelling to reveal a fourteenth century wall painting, discovered behind it during restoration. The bare stone wall with its faded religious message makes a sharp contrast to the style in which the clergy of Sterne's period lived, and the curious fact of it having lain hidden there, a secret, unknown behind the panelling for so many years, serves to add piquancy to one's view of it.

Two Stones and a Question of Dates

Across the village street from Shandy Hall the remains of Laurence Sterne lie beside the church where he served so happily in the last years of his life. Sterne died in London in 1768 and was interred in the burial ground of St. George's church Hanover Square. When that burial ground was cleared for development in 1969 his remains were brought to Coxwold for reburial. There had been stories of his body having been taken from the grave by body-snatchers but being recognised on the dissection table, hastily returned. Some doubts are therefore cast as to whether the remains were truly his, but the Sterne Trust is as confident as it is possible to be that the bones which now lie in Coxwold churchyard are indeed Sterne's.

To the east of the porch will be seen not one but two gravestones commemorating him and those who study them closely will see an interesting discrepancy with regard to his death. The upright stone against the wall gives his date of death as 13th September 1768 whilst the one lying flat on the ground gives the correct date 18th March 1768. One wonders how a mistake with such a wide discrepancy could have been made.

The Altar rail, Coxwold church

An unusual feature within the church of St. Michael at Coxwold is the altar rail dating probably from about 1760. Instead of the straight rail across the Chancel to be seen in churches as a general rule, the richly polished dark wood rail at Coxwold is in the form of an elongated U-shape. This unusual construction is a necessity in order to provide sufficient space for communicants to kneel at the rail to receive the Sacrament, because of the size and number of monuments within the Chancel.

There are other items of interest in the church, including the somewhat irreverent old roof bosses, and in a glass case near the Chancel arch a 'breeches' bible, so called because in the story of Adam and Eve they are described as covering themselves with breeches instead of the more usual version which says that they covered themselves with aprons of fig leaves.

The lectern was carved by Joseph Heu, an Austrian sculptor who fled from the Nazi occupation of his country and settled with his family during the Second World War, in the nearby village of Ampleforth.

In the floor of the central aisle of the Nave is a brass memorial to Sir John Manston who died in 1464. The name of his wife Elizabeth with space for the date of her death is also recorded there, but since the space still remains blank, it would appear that she has yet to join him. An unusually long life indeed! Unfortunately the glass protecting the brass has become yellow and cloudy and it is almost impossible to decipher the inscription.

At the rear of the church is a skilfully executed model of the church, made in order to raise funds for restoration, from more than 11,000 matchsticks.

Shandy Hall
Photograph by Eileen Rennison

The Altar rail, Coxwold church – Photograph by Eileen Rennison

Two stones and a question of dates
Photograph by Eileen Rennison

12. CROPTON

The New Inn

On the Pickering to Helmsley A170 turn right approximately 2½ miles from Pickering. Cropton is about 2¼ miles further on.

It is possible that many visitors to Cropton will be there because of the Roman Cawthorne Camps which are considered unique amongst Roman remains. It is also possible that they could completely overlook a most unusual feature of this small village by failing to visit the *New Inn*. They would be well advised however to call there and sample the local brew, Cropton Forest Gold.

Once beer was brewed everywhere on the premises of public houses, just as it was on isolated farms and in monastic institutions, but with the growth of the big breweries and easy transport making deliveries possible to once inaccessible places deep in the country, the public houses gradually dropped the brewing side of their business.

The *New Inn* at Cropton is unusual in that Cropton Forest Gold is not just brewed locally but actually right there on the premises in the old tradition of a public house.

It is something not to be missed; to be savoured not only for its rarity value, but also on its own merits.

The New Inn – Photograph by Richard Hebblethwaite

13. DALBY

Turf Maze

Some 8 miles out of Malton on the B1257 take a sharp left turn to Sheriff Hutton and York, immediately before turning into the village street at Hovingham. At a T junction about 3 miles along this road take the right turn to Dalby – NOT left to Terrington.

The only surviving example in North Yorkshire of an ancient game can be seen beside the quiet country road which leads from Terrington to Dalby and beyond to join the road to Helmsley. Through Dalby itself and past the turning to Skewsby a white railing protects the well-cut circular maze on the broad grass verge on the righthand side of the road.

The rules and origins of the game have long been lost, but 'treading the maze' was once a common regular entertainment of town and village life. Shakespeare made mention of it in 1594 when he had Titania complain to Oberon in 'A Midsummer Night's Dream', "*The nine men's morris is filled up with mud, And the quaint mazes in the wanton green, For lack of tread are indistinguishable.*"

The mazes are given different names in different parts of the country: Mismaze, Julian's Bower, Robin Hood's Race, Shepherd's Ring, Walls of Troy, Troy Town or City of Troy, the latter being the one by which this particular example has always been known. In some cathedrals and churches in France, and also occasionally in this country, a maze was used in patterns on the floor and elsewhere, adopting it as a symbol of life with its trials, leading eventually to Jerusalem, the name given to the centre of the maze, and the happy reward of the virtuous. Examples of mazes used in this way and known to the writer, are in the church at Alkborough near Goole, but on the southern bank of the river, and, further afield, on a roof boss in St. Mary Redcliffe church in Bristol.

Turf Maze
Photograph by Richard Hebblethwaite

14. EBBERSTON

The Smallest Stately Home

5 miles out of Pickering on the A170 road to Scarborough, Ebberston Hall stands on the left of the road about ½ mile before the village of Ebberston.

Ebberston Hall is a tiny Palladian mansion which has been described as the smallest stately home in England. It was built in 1718 for William Thompson, Member of Parliament for Scarborough and Master of the Mint for Queen Anne. It is said that the house was intended as an inducement to win him the love of a certain woman, but as far as is known she never even visited it. A century later it was owned by George Osbaldeston, the Regency eccentric who gambled away most of his money and earned for himself the title of the 'Sporting Squire of England', because of his interest and excellence in many sports.

The Grade One listed building was described by its architect as 'a Rustick Edifice' and has only eleven rooms in all. Squire Osbaldeston pulled down its two small wings intending to build larger ones but could never afford to do so, and in the early nineteen hundreds Sir Kenelm Cayley dismantled the cupola in order to sell the lead. Nevertheless the house remains an elegant perfectly proportioned miniature of classic architecture. In 1941 it became the property of the de Wend Fenton family who have striven to maintain and preserve it, opening it to the public each year between Easter and September.

The smallest Stately Home
Photograph by Richard Hebblethwaite

15. EGTON BRIDGE

The Mass House

From the A169 across the Moors turn left to Grosmont about 14½ miles out of Pickering. Continue through Grosmont and Egton to Egton Bridge, a distance of approximately 5 miles.

St. Hedda's Roman Catholic church at Egton Bridge is a large and imposing one with interesting relief panels on its outside wall depicting scenes from the life of Jesus, and inside, the Stations of the Cross also in the form of reliefs. A shrine in the church to Father Nicholas Postgate contains a crucifix, a pair of candlesticks, a missal and priest's vestment, together with other relics taken from his secret chapel.

Father Postgate said Mass and conducted ceremonies of the Roman Catholic faith when it was forbidden by law and Roman Catholics were persecuted for their religion. Born at Egton Bridge about 1597 he died in 1679 aged eighty-two, hung, drawn and quartered on the Knavesmire at York, after being betrayed for baptising a child.

He had been ordained abroad in 1628 and returned to England where he served surreptitiously as chaplain to various landed families, until at the age of sixty he returned to his native North York Moors to serve the poor as their priest. Despite his age he tramped the moors in all weathers, conducting services in secret, notices of which were conveyed in pre-arranged signals by means of sheets drying on the hedgerows, a method of drying washing once common amongst country folk.

Retracing one's steps and leaving Egton Bridge on the road to Egton there is an attractive red-roofed cottage with the unusual name of Mass House. It is on the right-hand side of the road, past the Cleveland Girl Guides house and the church, and being set back from the road on a slight rise it is easy to miss it as one is travelling in the opposite direction, into Egton Bridge.

The original Mass House was a low thatched building which unfortunately had deteriorated to such a bad state as to be beyond repair, and in 1928 had to be demolished. In 1830 however, a wall in the old original Mass House had collapsed, revealing Father Postgate's hidden chapel there ...a small loft still containing an altar made ready for the Mass. His congregation heard the Mass from the kitchen below, and a secret exit in the roof at the rear of the house meant that the Father could make a speedy escape should it become necessary. The present building which was erected on the site of the old Mass House, has a carved name stone on its end wall commemorating as nearly as possible the position of the secret chapel.

One cannot leave Egton Bridge without mention of an event held every year on the first Tuesday in August which can surely be regarded as a curious and unusual one — namely its famous Gooseberry Show at which gooseberries as big as golf balls and bigger, are the norm.

The Mass House – Photograph by Eileen Rennison

16. FLAXTON

Grazing Rights

Flaxton lies off the A64 York to Malton road. Take a left turn about 7 miles out of York and the village is about 1 mile from the main road.

On the moors sheep are a commonplace sight, not just on the moorland itself but also on the unfenced roads, necessitating extra care in driving along them. In the village of Flaxton eight miles from York the motorist is liable to be faced with a somewhat more surprising sight. He or she may find, not a sheep or lamb crossing their path, but the huge bulk of a slowly ambling cow, or indeed of a small herd of cows. They are not, as one might be excused for supposing, escapees from a nearby field. In fact, ancient rights allow them to graze on the broad village green and grass verges, and with cattle grids at every exit from the village to prevent them from straying too far, they wander freely and add an unusual touch to a pleasant little village; one not to be seen I believe anywhere else in the area.

Grazing Rights – Photograph by Eileen Rennison

17. FOSTON

A Famous Rector

About 5 miles from Malton on the A64 to York, turn off right to Foston which lies approximately 1½ miles further on.

Many visitors flock to see Castle Howard, featured by the writer Evelyn Waugh in his novel *Brideshead Revisited* and popularised by the television version of his work. Nearby is the quiet little village of Foston, a contrast to the grandeur of Castle Howard, but also with a literary association of which it is very proud.

Here that great man of letters, Sydney Smith, noted wit and advocate of radical reforms both social and religious, spent twenty-two years of his life. He was Rector in this quiet country parish from 1807 to 1829, despite his saying that he had 'no relish for the country. It is a kind of healthy grave', and 'in the country I always fear that creation will expire before tea-time'.

It is not easy to imagine this man of learning, founder of the *Edinburgh Review* and lecturer in Moral Philosophy, in such humble surroundings, but as a welcome guest at Castle Howard and in County Society, he no doubt enjoyed the finer things in life which were otherwise not so readily available in his previously neglected parish. He cared for his parish with genuine interest and worked hard for the improvement and welfare of his parishioners, and is remembered in the little village church by a handsome bronze memorial bearing his portrait in profile and an inscription praising his many virtues both as the village's Rector and as a man.

He had the sounding board added to the 15th century pulpit so that his words would carry throughout the church. On either side of the door are two prayer boards, a common enough feature of the 18th or early 19th centuries, but these particular boards are uncommon in that they contain a mistake — a repeated word — unnoticed or ignored at the time. Perhaps the craftsman in concentrating on the act of forming the letters lost the sense of the words, but it is amusing to speculate on whether Sydney Smith, who had such skill with words, ever read them and if so what his reaction would have been. A kind man, he no doubt decided to ignore the mistake, relying, with the words being so familiar, on the human tendency to read what one expects to see.

Sydney Smith memorial, All Saints Church, Foston
Photograph by Eileen Rennison.

18. FYLINGTHORPE

A Temple for Pigs, at Fyling Hall

About 3½ miles out of Whitby on the A171 road to Scarborough turn off left to Fylingthorpe, about 2 miles. Fyling Hall lies about 1 mile to the right. Continue past the Hall (school) on the narrow road to where a row of cottages stands at right angles to the road. The Pigsty is at the far end of the row.

The pigsty built in 1883 by Squire John Walter Barry at Fyling Hall near Robin Hood's Bay to house his two favourite sows, has a double claim to being unusual. Firstly, the architectural style for a pigsty is sumptuous and uncommon to say the least. Squire Barry obviously felt that his pigs deserved only the very best of environments; or it may be that he was simply moved by the fashion of the time for elaborate and whimsical follies, to enhance the landscape of his estate. He was much given to travelling abroad and often brought back with him new plants and trees and architectural ideas. Whatever his reason for it the result was a pigsty in the form of a small Greek temple, complete with Doric columns, decorated in ochre, gold and red. Whether the delightful visual aspects of their dwelling with its distant view of the sea favourably affected the eccentric squire's pigs in any way we do not know.

But in its second claim to the unusual they will surely be a source of pleasure to its future occupants, for the one-time pigsty has now been converted, with the addition of modern comforts and conveniences, into a holiday home.

Certainly one of the oddest of pigsties and now one of the most unusual of holiday homes. The front of the building can only be seen across the fields from the road, but from the road behind the cottages a closer view of the back can be seen.

A Temple for Pigs – Photographs by Eileen Rennison.

25

19. GILLAMOOR

Four Faces

Some 7 miles from Pickering on the A170 to Helmsley take the turning to Kirkbymoorside and continue for about 3 miles to Gillamoor.

Just a few miles from Appleton-le-Moors in the village of Gillamoor, faces are once again a feature of the main street. These however, are not human faces but of a totally different kind; namely the faces of an unusual sundial, remarkable not in themselves but in their number.

Sundials, the only means of telling the time before the invention of clocks and watches, are devices of great antiquity. This particular one dates back a mere hundred and ninety-three years to 1800 and was provided by public subscription. It is set into a recess of the garden wall of the farmhouse to which it gives the name Dial House Farm. Of quite considerable size, it consists of a high stepped plinth and a central column surmounted by a block with a dial face on each of its four sides. Many sundials bear an inscription, often in Latin, referring to the fleeting passage of time, or a warning of man's mortality. There are inscriptions here, but because of weathering and moss, I was quite unable to discover the nature of them; others may perhaps be more successful than I.

One should not leave Gillamoor without taking in the superb view of Lower Farndale which can be seen from the corner by the village church. Known as Surprise View, its breath-taking beauty has inspired the inscription on the churchyard wall of a verse by John Keble, the 19th century Oxford professor of poetry and hymn writer, after whom Keble College, Oxford was named.

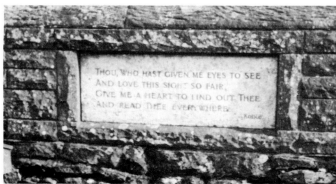

Four Faces – Photographs by Eileen Rennison

26

20. GLAISDALE

Beggar's Bridge

About 14½ miles from Pickering on the A169 to Whitby take the turning to Grosmont and Egton, and continue to Glaisdale, a distance of about 7 miles.

There are many narrow, elegantly arched pack-horse bridges set in idyllic surroundings throughout Yorkshire, but none surely can have a more romantic history than the so-called Beggar's Bridge spanning the River Esk at Glaisdale.

Legend has it that Tom Ferres, a local lad, used to wade or swim across the river to meet his sweetheart in secret. When her father found out, he would not hear of Tom as a suitor for his daughter because of his lack of wealth or prospects. However, he did not rule out all possibility of a marriage between the young couple at some future date and different circumstances. Tom went away vowing that he would make his fortune, return to claim his bride and build a bridge across the Esk where he had so often had a wetting.

He went first to sea on a Whitby boat that took part in the defeat of the Armada. Later, after an apprenticeship to a Hull shipowner, he was able to buy a vessel of his own and soon became a very wealthy man. In 1620 as a man of great standing and influence in the town, he was honoured with the office of Mayor of Hull and Admiral of the Humber. As an Elder Brother of Hull Trinity House, he presented to them the old Carmelite Friary at Hull to build new premises, for which he had paid 'one thousand two hundred broad pieces'. He also presented a silver cup and a silver salt to the Corporation, both of which remain amongst its treasures.

But before that he had old pledges to fulfil. He had never forgotten his old sweetheart, or his promise when scarcely more than a 'beggar' to build a bridge so that others might cross freely at his old river crossing place. He returned to Glaisdale to marry his sweetheart, and his bridge still stands bearing his initials 'T.F.' and the date 1619; a solid and beautiful memorial to lasting love and loyalty.

Beggar's Bridge
Photograph by Richard Hebblethwaite

21. GOATHLAND

Wade's Causeway, Wheeldale Moor

On the A169 Pickering to Whitby road, take the turning to Goathland approximately 11 miles out of Pickering. On reaching Goathland – approximately 3 miles distance – do not enter the village street but turn left, and about ¾ mile further on this road turn left again. Continue for about 1 mile to Hunt House where the car must be left and the path taken on foot to the Roman Road.

Although many modern roads follow the lines of their Roman counterparts, there are only two places in England where an actual stretch of Roman road has been preserved and restored to a state more or less as it was originally built. One of these is the mile long stretch across Wheeldale Moor.

Known as Wade's Causeway after the legendary giant of these parts, who is said to have single-handedly formed the nearby Hole of Horcum by scooping up a handful of soil, the road crosses the moor from Wheeldale Bridge towards Goathland. It dates from the end of the first century and is an impressive monument to the remarkable skill and knowledge of the Roman engineers who built it across the wild and inhospitable countryside so long ago.

The road is raised one to two feet above the ground and shows clearly the details and foundations of its structure. Side drains carried off surplus water, making it passable in winter. The surface is roughly paved but would have been coverd originally with gravel or small stones. The width is such as to allow for two normal sized waggons or ten marching Roman legionaries. Running north-east from Cawthorne Training Camps, it connected the Roman Fort at Malton with the coastal signal stations in the area around Whitby.

It is possible to feel here on the moor, the unique experience of walking along the same road that Roman feet once trod, by taking just a short drive from Goathland followed by a short walk on to the moor.

An Anchor in the Churchyard

A large chain and anchor in the churchyard at Goathland, suggests that it might mark the grave of some native seafarer perhaps lost at sea. Oddly, however, there appears to be no romantic history attached to it and it bears merely the names and dates of Mr. and Mrs. Jefferick whom it commemorates. Nevertheless it is an unusual sight in this quiet moorland graveyard, evoking connotations of a ship brought finally to rest, at anchor after its journey over a restless sea.

*Wade's Causeway
Photograph by
Richard Hebblethwaite.*

*An anchor in the churchyard
Photograph by
Eileen Rennison.*

22. GREAT AYTON

Cook Family Gravestone

Follow the B1257 Helmsley to Stokesley road for some 20 miles to a roundabout. Here take the A173 to Great Ayton, a distance of about 2¼ miles. Turn left across the bridge, and sharp left along the river bank a very short distance to the church on the right. The grave is to the right of the path in the graveyard straight ahead.

Great Ayton is the village where Captain Cook, the explorer and discoverer of Australia, went to school. He was born at Marton near Middlesbrough but left there with his parents at the age of eight.

The village contains many reminders of Cook's fame and there is much to interest the visitor. His old school-room is now a small museum, and an obelisk marks the spot where his parents' retirement cottage stood, although the cottage itself was dismantled, shipped and re-erected in Australia in 1934. A second obelisk on the top of the nearby Easby Hill is a monument to Cook himself.

But the visitor looking for the unusual should not fail to visit the churchyard of All Saints, where the explorer's mother and five of his brothers and sisters are buried. Their gravestone is believed to have been carved by Cook's father himself and is distinguished by the oddly expressed record it bears of his brother William's age — two years, twelve months, sixteen days and seven hours. In contrast he seems to have been in some doubt about the year of death and has solved the problem as to whether it was 1747 or 1748 by giving it as 174⅞.

The other side of the stone tells of Captain Cook's own death and shows an unusual spelling to modern eyes of Hawaii.

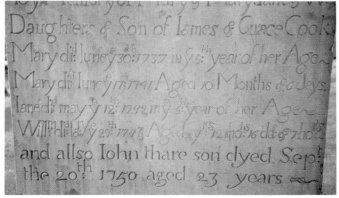

Cook's family Gravestone – Photographs by Eileen Rennison.

23. HELMSLEY

Greek Temples and a Record Tree

Helmsley is 13 miles west of Pickering on the A170 and 16 miles north-west of Malton on the B1257.

Helmsley is an attractive, busy market town well loved by visitors. As well as its popular Friday market it has interesting features and historic places to visit.

Helmsley Castle, now ruined, was built in 1186 and during the Civil War withstood a siege of three months. It has an interesting architectural plan with its keep built into the outer wall.

Duncombe Park, the seat of the Earl of Feversham, is also situated in Helmsley. It was built in 1713, in the style of Vanburgh who built Castle Howard, by an amateur architect named Wakefield, but was twice damaged by fires and rebuilt in the original style. The house, gardens and parkland are now open to the public, but for many years the house was occupied by a private school for girls. It has been extensively refurbished by the present Earl in order to open it to the public. The main feature of the gardens is the long grass terrace looking down on to the River Rye, with its small Greek temples, one at either end, one Doric, one Ionic.

The visitor who takes a stroll along the woodland walk should keep an eye open for the tallest ash tree in England, there beside the path, marked by a plaque and recorded in the Guinness Book of Records 1965 — 1974.

Record Tree
Photograph by Eileen Rennison

24. HELMSLEY BANK
Controversial Sculpture on Roppa Edge

In Helmsley take the road past the church and the Feversham Arms. After about 200 yards follow the No Through Road indicated to the left for about 4 miles. Remembering to close gates.

The traveller who takes the road out of Helmsley leading to Helmsley Bank is rewarded by splendid views and lovely scenery. This is only to be expected as the whole of this area is one of special beauty. More of a surprise is the sight of a piece of modern sculpture out there in the countryside.

In 1977, the sculpture by the York sculptor Austin Wright was installed there to a chorus of protests, conflicting views and controversy in the local papers. For some people its modern design was to be deplored, while for others its location was the point of contention. One would expect that the years and familiarity must surely have mellowed local opinion towards this work of art, and the damage, when last seen, that it has sadly suffered, is the result of mindless vandalism.

Sculpture is best seen as part of a landscape or townscape in which it can take its place in space which allows an all-round view and the possibility of both a long view and a close view. The simple large empty frames of this particular sculpture seem eminently suited to the wide open spaces, and contain and focus the eye on parts of the scenery spread before one. The contrast between the man-made object and the work of Nature serves to highlight and enhance the visual pleasure given by both.

Controversial Sculpture
Photograph by
Richard Hebblethwaite

25. HINDERWELL

St. Hilda's Well

Hinderwell is on the A174 between Whitby and Loftus and 10 miles out of Whitby. At the end of the village, take the right turn signposted to Port Mulgrave, then almost immediately left for the church .

Hinderwell would seem to be an unremarkable village centred around the main road from Whitby to Loftus, but the traveller who pauses there instead of hurrying through, will find that it contains one unusual feature, one which is said to have given the village its name.

At the end of the village the church stands in splendid isolation high on a triangular island of green surrounded by roads. There among the gravestones, and at first not easily distinguishable from them, is St. Hilda's well. It is not a well in the sense of a deep sunken shaft, but in the archaic sense of a spring or fount in the slope of the ground, protected by stone slabs.

St. Hilda, Abbess of Hartlepool, who founded the Abbey at Whitby in 657 and was its Abbess until her death in 680, was said by some to have had a cell here at Hinderwell to which she could retire for meditation. Others claim only that she rested and refreshed herself at the well on her journeys through the area.

Subsequent corruption over the years, of Hilda's well, leading to the name of Hinderwell seems plausible enough, but whether you believe in the legend or not, or whether you think perhaps Hinderwell has some derivation from its being in the hinder or hinterland from the coast, in the quiet of the graveyard behind the church, the traffic on the roads out of sight, the only sound the cawing of the rooks in the nearby trees, it is not too difficult to imagine the Abbess refreshing herself at the well and blessing it. Like many such Holy wells there may

have been claims of curative powers for the water, and like many others in Derbyshire and elsewhere, the well is 'dressed' with flowers by the children of Hinderwell.

St. Hilda's Well
Photographs by Eileen Rennison.

26. THE HOLE OF HORCUM

The Hole of Horcum lies on the left of the A169 road to Whitby about 8 miles from Pickering. A large parking space is situated on the opposite side of the road.

The hollow basin of the Hole of Horcum at Saltersgate between Pickering and Whitby is an unexpected and surprising geological feature to find in this landscape. Indeed, it is difficult to believe that it is not a man-made excavation, but it is in fact a natural phenomenon, formed over thousands of years by the effects of water erosion into the moor.

The legendary version of its formation however, is that the local giant Wade, in a rage with his wife, took up a handful of earth and flung it at her; his aim being poor — no doubt his rage being too great for accuracy — he missed her and the clod of earth fell not far away to form a rounded hill. Thus Wade is credited not only with the creation of the Hole of Horcum but also of Blakey Topping.

Whatever you choose to believe about it, it is still an odd and somewhat awesome view as one stands on the rim and gazes down into the crater of the Hole. How much more so it must be for the hang-gliders who in these modern days are able to hover and swoop over and down into it.

Hole of Horcum
Photograph by Richard Hebblethwaite.

33

27. HOVINGHAM

Hovingham Hall

Hovingham is 8 miles from Malton on the B1257 road to Helmsley.

Hovingham Hall stands behind the green at the very heart of the village of Hovingham, and was the home before her marriage, of Katherine Worsley, now the Duchess of Kent. It was built by Thomas Worsley between 1752 and 1769, to a most unusual and idiosyncratic architectural design.

Thomas Worsley was acknowledged to be one of the best riders of his day and was passionately fond of horses. So much so that he planned his house in such a way that his horses were also actually housed within it on the ground floor. Entry is through the riding school to the front door which leads, not as one might expect into a spacious and elegant hallway, but directly into the vaulted stables.

The Grand Ballroom which is situated above the stables has a balcony which overlooks the riding school. From there the guests in their fine clothes could watch the horses being schooled and trained below — an extra diversion, no doubt adding to an evening's pleasure.

One does wonder whether such a curious and unusual arrangement, with rooms of the house over the stables, might not have its disadvantages particularly in hot weather. To Thomas Worsley however, with his great love for his horses, the sounds of them and the inevitable 'horsy' smells, can only have been an added pleasure, one supposes.

The Hall is not open to the general public, but because of its situation in the centre of the village and its lack of the usual long driveway, it is quite possible to appreciate its unusual features to some degree from the roadway at its entrance.

Hovingham School

Opposite the entrance to the Hall, on the village green, is Hovingham village school, which can also lay claim to an unusual architectural feature; namely an oriel window of remarkable size, quite disproportionate to the little building itself. It is built in a style which could be seen by many as ugly, and indeed it has been described by that chronicler of architecture throughout the land, Sir Nicholas Pevsner, as 'truly hideous'. To others, however, it may seem merely out-of-the-ordinary and quaint; an unusually opulent type of window to be found on a small village school.

Hovingham Hall
Photograph by Richard Hebblethwaite

Hovingham School
Photograph by Eileen Rennison

28. HUTTON-LE-HOLE

Witch Posts

Hutton-le-Hole is 9 miles from Pickering and a similar distance from Helmsley, off the A170, taking a right turn about 6½ miles out of Pickering. The Ryedale Folk Museum is in the main village street where there is no parking. A large car park is provided at the end of the village. The Museum is open daily 10.30 – 17.30 from Easter to October.

Witch posts would seem to be almost exclusively a feature of the North York Moors. Of known examples, eighteen have come from the Moors area, the odd one out being one from the nearby county of Lancashire. There may well be others as yet undiscovered in cottages throughout the area, for as recently as 1984 a cottage which contained one was sold near Pickering. Others have been discovered in the past at Farndale, Rosedale, Gillamoor, Egton and Lealholm. The Pitt-Rivers Museum in Oxford and the Whitby Museum contain examples, but perhaps best of all is the one to be seen in the Ryedale Folk Museum at Hutton-le-Hole, It originated in a house in Danby, but because it is now part of a reconstructed cottage in the museum, it is shown to greater advantage in its natural setting, rather than in isolation as a single museum exhibit.

A witch post, as the name implies, is a solid upright timber of oak or rowan wood (both of which trees are credited with magical powers) which is built in as part of the house's structure. The most usual place to find one is by the fireplace, supporting the smoke hood. Its distinguishing mark is a carved cross near the top of the post. As well as this simple cross there may be other symbols whose meanings are not always clear to us today. Some posts bear initials or a date from the seventeenth century; a period which believed in witchcraft and the power of witches.

However, despite their name there is no irrefutable evidence which can be put forward to support the idea that their purpose was indeed to protect the house and its inhabitants from witches. The seventeenth century was also a time of religious intolerance, and it has been suggested that perhaps intinerant priests who were sheltered there gave a blessing on the house and its occupants, and the occasion was recorded by the carving of a cross on these wooden posts.

Whatever may be the true reason for their origin, they are traditionally known by the name of witch posts and remain a unique and intriguing feature of this part of Yorkshire.

Witch Post - Ryedale Folk Museum
Photograph by Eileen Rennison.

29. KILBURN

The White Horse

The Kilburn White Horse can be approached in three ways. From the A170 from Helmsley to Thirsk, about 7½ miles from Helmsley, just past the Hambleton Hotel, take a left turn along a narrow and steep road, past the Gliding Club to the car park at the foot of the Horse. A total distance of roughly 9 miles.

Alternatively continue a further ½ mile along the A170 to the Sutton Bank Visitor centre and car park. From there it is possible to walk along the cliff top past the Gliding Club to the Horse. A walk of 1½ to 2 miles over fairly rough paths.

If approaching from the A19 York to Thirsk road turn off right just through Easingwold to Husthwaite and then Coxwold to Kilburn, about 7½ miles from Easingwold. From Kilburn the road to the car park at the foot of the Horse snakes up the hill for approximately a further ¾ mile.

The White Horse
Photograph by Richard Hebblethwaite.

The White Horse cut into the one in four escarpment above the village of Kilburn is a popular and distinctive landmark. Simple and representational in appearance it is not of prehistoric origin like the Celtic style horse on the Berkshire Downs above Uffingham, though it was in fact inspired by it. It is one of the many intaglio hill-horses cut in the eighteenth and nineteenth centuries as a result of the growing interest in antiquities and the popularity of the anatomically exact paintings of George Stubbs, though few of these horses have survived.

The Yorkshire Horse was the idea of Thomas Taylor of Kilburn who left to make his fortune in business in London.

On a visit to the horse at Uffingham he visualised the impact such a landmark would make on Roulston Scar above his native village. Although his suggestion did not at first find favour, he eventually found an ally in John Hodgson the village schoolmaster, who took up the idea, drew up the plans and supervised the construction. With the help of his pupils and thirty-three men the horse was marked out, cut and cleared of scrub, and completed on 4th November 1857. The achievement of their huge creation was celebrated in the little village with a great feast, at which more than a hundred gallons of beer were drunk and two roasted bullocks were eaten.

The horse is larger than the ancient hill-horses, measuring three hundred and fourteen feet long and two hundred and twenty-eight feet high. Twenty people can comfortably stand on the eye and although nowadays walking on the horse is very much discouraged, it was popular in the writer's youth to climb the hill from Kilburn to picnic on the area of turf that forms the eye, enjoying the magnificent views over the Vale of York.

Today a road and car park provide easier access for visitors and steps beside the horse itself make the last lap possible for all but the very unfit or frail. It is really best seen from a distance as because of its size the closer one gets to it the more the horse becomes distorted until it finally 'disappears'. Perhaps the members of the nearby Gliding Club get the best view as they hover above, but viewing points have been claimed from as far as forty miles away in all directions.

Unlike other horses cut into chalk hills, the Kilburn Horse lies on soft limestone which is porous and easily disintegrates; nor does it give a more or less permanent white surface as chalk does. Six tons of lime were originally used to whiten the surface but constant weathering and erosion make frequent resurfacing necessary. At two or three yearly intervals, with the help of volunteers the horse has been restored with limestone and yellow chalk chippings which weather to a brilliant white. The steepness of the hill makes delivery of materials and working conditions extremely difficult, but various different groups of young people have continued to rise to the challenge. The most recent whitening of the surface, in 1992, has been achieved by the application of three tonnes of the type of marking paint used on sports fields, generously donated, together with the specially adapted means of application, by a firm which manufactures it.

With their long associations with horse-racing the Hambleton Hills make an appropriate setting for the White Horse; a fact which could have influenced Thomas Taylor in his idea. It is a unique feature not only in this area but indeed in the North of England, as other hill-horses exist mainly in the more southerly parts of the country, and whether so intended or not, it stands as a symbol of the traditional Yorkshire love and knowledge of horses.

30. KIRKDALE

Saxon Sundial, St. Gregory's Minster

On the A170 Helmsley to Pickering road take a left turn signposted to St. Gregory's Minster about 3½ miles from Helmsley. The church is a further distance of about ¾ mile.

Many old churches in the Vale of Pickering have carved crosses and old stones of Celtic and Saxon design built into their walls. St. Gregory's Minster, Kirkdale, is set in romantic isolation in the lovely valley of the Hodge Beck; one of the oldest and most interesting churches in England, it has the almost unique feature and great treasure of a large and remarkably preserved Saxon sundial. This can be seen inside the porch over the south doorway and records the rebuilding of the church in the reign of Edward the Confessor. It is seven feet long and two feet wide and divided into three panels. It is interesting to note that the dial in the centre panel is divided into only eight hours. Above the dial an inscription reads *'This is the day's sun marker at every time'*. The wording of the side panels, when translated into modern language says, 'Orm Gamal's son bought St. Gregory's Minster when it was all broken down and fallen and he let it be made new from the ground to Christ and to St. Gregory in the days of Edward the King and of Tosti the Earl. And Harwarth me wrought and Brand priest'. This information makes it possible to date the sundial and the building to between 1055 and 1065. The inscriptions are not difficult to decipher in spite of the Northumbrian English and some runic characters. It may be interesting to compare other small and less clear Saxon sundials in the area, at Great Edstone and Old Byland.

St. Gregory's Minster

Saxon Sundial
Photographs by Eileen Rennison.

31. LASTINGHAM

The Shrine of St. Cedd

About 6½ miles from Pickering on the A170 Pickering to Helmsley road take a right turn to Hutton-le-Hole. In the village take a right turn and follow the road over the moor to Lastingham, a total distance of about 10 ¾ miles. The church is on the right as one enters Lastingham.

It is not usual for a parish church to have a crypt and the small moorland village of Lastingham seems an unlikely place to find this unique feature; yet the parish church of St. Mary contains an apsidal crypt virtually unchanged for nearly a thousand years: the only surviving example in the country, with Chancel, Nave and Aisles forming a small church in itself.

The explanation for this unexpected and ancient crypt lies in the fact that Lastingham has been a centre of religion since the seventh century. It was the site of the Monastery of Lastingham founded in AD 659 by St. Cedd of Lindisfarne, Bishop of East Anglia, and his brother St. Chad, later Bishop of York and Lichfield, as we are told by the Venerable Bede in his *History of the English Church and People*. Cedd fell a victim to the plague, died and was buried at Lastingham.

The buildings of his monastery were in all probability destroyed by the invading Danes in the ninth or tenth century. In 1078 Stephen, the Abbot of Whitby, rebuilt the monastery and built the crypt as a shrine to St. Cedd, who lies buried beside the altar there.

The monks of Whitby did not remain long at Lastingham but withdrew because of the danger from marauders to found St. Mary's Abbey at York. The present church at Lastingham was completed in 1228, built on the foundations of Stephen's great Abbey Church, which he never completed. Over the years it has been added to and has seen some restoration as all churches do.

Legend has it that in the eighteenth century the crypt was used for cock-fighting, but to stand in the peace of the crypt today is a unique experience and one cannot fail to be awed by the sense of history and the realisation that one is standing in the very place where these ancient saints have been.

The Crypt
Photograph by Eileen Rennison.

32. LITTLEBECK

The Hermitage

Approximately 16 miles from Pickering on the A169 road to Whitby, turn right down the steep road to Littlebeck about 1¾ miles. There is a car park at the village hall. Proceeding on foot turn left along the road a short distance to Littlebeck Wood on the right. Enter by the gate and the Hermitage is about 1 mile.

One of the North York Moors' many splendid waterfalls, Falling Foss, is to be found in the small secluded valley of the Little Beck off the Pickering to Whitby road. Not far from the waterfall is the curious so-called Hermitage.

A large boulder hollowed out to form a shelter with a gothic pointed doorway and stone seating, it was the work of a sailor named Jeffery, for the local schoolmaster George Chubb, whose initials and the date 1790 appear on it. This man-made cave was part of a scheme to enhance the grounds of Newton House nearby, for the benefit of a new owner, Jonas Brown. It is an example of the popularity at the time of such 'follies' with many landed gentlemen actually going so far as to install and support their own resident hermit.

There is a splendid position for viewing from the outside of the Hermitage. After seeing this man-made curiosity the visitor may like to continue further along the way and take in the natural splendour of Falling Foss.

The Hermitage
Photograph by Richard Hebblethwaite.

33. MOORLAND CROSSES

Ralph Cross is beside the road from Hutton-le-Hole to Westerdale. Take the road straight through Hutton-le-Hole and the Cross lies to the left after about 8½ miles or 3 miles from Westerdale.

Lilla Cross lies on Fylingdale Moor approximately 2¾ miles from the road to the right at Ellerbeck Bridge about 10¾ miles out of Pickering on the A169 to Whitby.

For Fat Betty follow the road to Rosedale from near Ralph Cross for about ½ mile.

Ancient stone crosses abound on the North York Moors, indeed they are so much a feature of this area that one of them — Ralph Cross — has been adopted as the symbol and logo of the National Park. Of Medieval origin, their purpose is somewhat surrounded in mystery. It is possible that some were placed simply to mark out the boundaries of parishes or other territories, or that they were intended to serve as navigational guides to travellers along ancient routes across the treacherous moors. Whatever their purpose their solitary and enigmatic presence seems to typify the nature of the moors.

One whose purpose we do know is Lilla Cross, the oldest of all the moorland crosses, which stands on the prehistoric track known as Old Wife's Trod, above Lilla Howe. In AD 626 the King of the West Saxons sent an assassin to kill Edwin King of Northumbria, whose kingdom stretched from the Humber to the Scottish borders. The assassin struck as Edwin was journeying across Fylingdale Moor, but Lilla, who was in attendance on the King, saved his life by protecting him with his own body and was himself stabbed to death with the poisoned sword. The cross is a memorial to Lilla who was a Christian. Edwin himself became a Christian as a result of Lilla's brave sacrifice and built a stone church at York, a forerunner of the Minster.

One of the best known of the crosses is White Cross, marking the conjunction of the parish boundaries of Danby, Rosedale and Westerdale. Popularly known as Fat Betty it is aptly named, being a squat white stone with a wheel-head top. Stump Cross at Brown Rigg End is another stone very similar in appearance to Fat Betty.

Old Ralph – Photograph by Richard Hebblethwaite

Ralph Cross stands high on Westerdale Moor at the crossroads leading to Castleton, Hutton-le-Hole and Rosedale. This cross is often referred to as Young Ralph and a few hundred yards to the south-west is the smaller cross known as Old Ralph.

A fifty-three mile walk starting and finishing at Goathland, takes in thirteen of the best known of the moorland crosses. The route includes Botton Cross, Fat Betty, the Ralph Crosses, Ana Cross, High Cross and Low cross, Mauley Cross, Malo Cross, and Lilla Cross, Postgate Cross, John Cross and York Cross. It is an annual challenge pioneered by Malcolm Boyes who has written a paperback *The Crosses Walk* published by the *Dalesman*.

Such a walk is only for the really hardy and the seasoned walker, but fortunately it is quite possible to enjoy the sight of one or more of these curious outstanding features of the moorland landscape with considerably less effort, on foot or by car.

Fat Betty
Photograph by Richard Hebblethwaite

Young Ralph
Photograph by Richard Hebblethwaite

34. NAWTON

An Unusual Bus-Shelter

Nawton is on the A170 road 10¼ miles from Pickering and 2¾ miles from Helmsley.

On the Scarborough to Helmsley road the two villages of Nawton and Beadlam are joined together as one, and at the point where they meet is an unusual shelter and memorial. It is built around an old sycamore tree, the trunk of which serves as its centre post. Octagonal in shape with the roof supported at its outer edges on sturdy wooden posts, and with wooden seats encircling the tree trunk, the shelter provides a welcome and comfortable cover for waiting bus passengers, as well as an interesting focus for the village. A memorial tablet shows that it was erected to the memory of a young boy, with the simple inscription:-

To the dear and happy memory of David Duncombe Born 8th February 1910. Died 8th September 1927.

Despite the nearness of Duncombe Park, home of the Earl of Feversham, there seems to be no family connection.

An unusual bus shelter
Photograph by
Richard Hebblethwaite

35. NETHER SILTON

A Mysterious Inscription

Going north on the A19 take a right turn about 6½ miles from Thirsk. Nether Silton is about a further 2 ¼ miles.

Alternatively, from Helmsley take the A170 down Sutton Bank, turn off at Sutton-under-Whitestone-Cliffe to Felixkirk, Kepwick and Nether Silton, approximately 20 miles.

At the edge of the National Park, off the A19 road to Northallerton, along a twisting and picturesque road, lies the secluded and attractive village of Nether Silton, and there in a field behind the church stands a solitary rough-hewn stone. The upright stone, about five feet in height, appears at first glance to be just a standing stone — an old gatepost even — but on closer inspection on one side is the mysterious inscription:

> HTGOMHS
> TBBWOTGWWG
> TWOTEWAHH
> ATCLABWHEY
> AD 1765
> AWPSAYAA

The explanation of this strange lettering is that it commemorates an old manor house and was carved for Silton's Squire Hickes in the eighteenth century; each letter is the initial only of a word and the translation runs as follows — *Here the grand old manor house stood. The black beams were oak the great walls were good. The walls of the east wing are hidden here. A thatched cottage like a barn was here erected year AD 1765. A wide porch spans a yard and alcove.*

The mystery remains however, as to why the Squire should choose such an enigmatic inscription to convey

A mysterious inscription
Photographs by Eileen Rennison.

36. OLDSTEAD

Mount Snever Observatory

From Helmsley take the A170 road to Thirsk. After about 4 miles turn left to Wass, Byland Abbey and then right to Oldstead, a distance of about a further 4 miles. At the end of the village, take the right turn marked "No Through Road", past the house with a turret to the gateway at the edge of the forest. Leave car. Take the forest track to the right for about ten minutes. A mossy bank on the left is the entry to a very narrow very steep path.

On the hill behind the village of Oldstead and between it and the nearby village of Wass, a tower can be seen rising above the trees of the Forestry plantation. It is known as Mount Snever Observatory, and once housed a large telescope and other astronomical instruments. It was built at the instigation of a John Wormald to commemorate the reign of the new monarch, Queen Victoria; a somewhat unusual place for a monument of an unusual type one might think.

There is no access to the tower today and the paths to it are not easy to locate. It is not for the casual walker, but for those with stout shoes and a detailed map it makes a pleasant excursion through the woods on the hillside.

There are several inscriptions on the building though they are not easy to read. Two of them give credit to the builder and to John Wormald. One contains a long verse in the course of which tribute is paid to Queen Victoria with a reference to industry on the plain and the words *peace and plenty tell Victoria reigns.* Since the tower was erected in the first year of her reign these words can only be of a hopeful anticipatory nature, rather than a comment on past record. Although elsewhere in Victoria's reign the word industry could have a different meaning, here in this rural landscape it could only refer to

diligence and hard work on the land. The countryside and the views from Mount Snever Observatory remain much the same today as they were then, and as the anonymous poet of the inscription also says:-

Happy the man who to these shades retires
Who Nature chains and whom the Muse inspires.

Mount Snever Observatory
Photograph by Eileen Rennison.

37. OSMOTHERLEY

3½ miles out of Helmsley on the B1257 road to Stokesley take a left turn to Hawnby, a further distance of 2½ miles. In Hawnby take the road to Osmotherley, 9 miles.

Alternatively, Osmotherley lies on the right about 1 mile off the A19 road to Northallerton about 10¼ miles from Thirsk. The entrance drive to Mount Grace Priory is signposted less than a mile beyond the turn to Osmotherley on the A19.

Chequers Inn.

The Old Drove Road runs for about fifteen miles within the National Park to the west of the Moors and along the ridge of Black Hambleton hill. It remains a broad grass track for some of those miles, as it was in the heyday of the large scale droving in the eighteenth and early nineteenth centuries from which it takes its name, when thousands of sheep and cattle were driven down from the north to markets as far away as Smithfield in London; but parts of it now coincide with our present day metalled roads.

The drovers on their long trek south obviously had need of regular stopping places along the road for rest and refreshment. One of these places was the old Chequers Inn, now a farm, on the moor edge a mile or so out of Osmotherley on the road to Hawnby.

The inn took its name from the tokens issued to the drovers to be exchanged there for refreshment. Though no longer the scene of the bustle and noise of the rough drovers it is still possible for the passing traveller to obtain refreshment there in the form of teas, home-made scones and ice-cream.

The tantalising old inn sign is still prominently displayed on the outside wall to tempt one with its invitation and easy promise —

> *Be not in haste – step in and taste*
> *Ale tomorrow for nothing.*

Mount Grace Priory. A very early serving hatch.

The monks of the Carthusian Order lived a life of manual work, study and prayer, isolated not only from the outside world, but for the most part also from each other. They gathered only in church and ate together in the Frater only on festivals. Consequently each monk required a separate house, and communal rooms such as dormitories were not a feature of their monasteries as they were of others.

At Mount Grace Priory, founded in 1398 at the foot of the hills close to Osmotherley, their way of life can be very clearly seen. The monks' cells or houses are ranged around the sides of the Cloisters, each set in its own small garden and each containing a living-room, a bedroom, a study and a workshop. At the bottom of each garden is a small 'garderobe' set over the main drain. But perhaps the most unexpected and telling feature of this solitary life is to be seen beside the doorway on the Cloister side of the cell. Set into the wall is a serving hatch so that meals may be brought for the monk inside. But this is no ordinary simple hatch such as we might find in a house today. Without doors and making a right-angled bend in the thickness of the wall, it enabled the server to place the food, and the inmate to retrieve it, without either being able to so much as catch a glimpse of the other.

Speaking to each other was forbidden in the Order, except on Sundays, but one cannot help wondering if a stolen whisper was exchanged sometimes through the hatches. Or how often food, placed silently within, grew cold before the inmate, perhaps deep in meditation or study, realised it was there.

Outdoor table and Pulpit

In many villages an old Market Cross can be seen. It is a not unusual feature. In Osmotherley however, one finds not only a stone column set on a small green at the centre of the village, but also beside it the more unusual sight of a stone 'barter table'. Here the goods could be displayed and examined and haggled over. And upon it John Wesley, on his travels through Yorkshire, is said to have stood to preach his open air sermon to the people, as was his custom. If so his words seem to have fallen on receptive ears, for tucked away in an alleyway off the main street opposite and not far from the barter table, is the Osmotherley Methodist Church dated 1754; surely one of the earliest established.

The visitor to Osmotherley should not leave without sampling the pleasure of another unusual, though totally different feature of the village. I refer to the splendid and renowned public toilets attached to the old Schoolroom. I can only speak from experience of the Ladies, but I am told that the Gentlemen are also housed in similar style. Where else in a public toilet can one find perfect cleanliness, shining tiles, pot plants, cut flowers, pictures and carpeting? Small wonder that the walls are decorated with messages and poems of appreciation from near and far.

Chequers Inn – Photographs by Eileen Rennison.

Mount Grace Priory
Photographs by Eileen Rennison.

Outdoor table and pulpit
Photograph by Eileen Rennison.

38. PICKERING

American Connections

Pickering lies on the A170 road 16 miles from Scarborough and 13 miles from Helmsley. It is 8 miles north of Malton on the A169.

The parish church of St. Peter and St. Paul at Pickering has many features of great interest, including some magnificent and extensive medieval wall paintings, accidentally uncovered in the mid-nineteenth century, and a memorial to William Marshall the eighteenth century rural economist whose importance to the development of agriculture is not always remembered or appreciated.

It is also notable however in a way more unexpected perhaps in such a small quiet market town, namely for its strong connections with the United States of America. In the Sanctuary an old memorial commemorates Robert King, born in Pickering in 1740 and buried there in 1817, and his son Nicholas. Both were surveyors who were leading figures in the planning of the American capital, the city of Washington. As well as the memorial tablet, maps and a picture at the rear of the Nave, also serve to illustrate this fact, from which later ties were to evolve.

Under the tablet to the Kings are brasses commemorating the American Alliance in 1917, and Ambassador Walter Hines Page. Donations from American citizens paid for panelling in the Choir and Chancel, also in memory of a former Ambassador Joseph H. Choate, and of Henry Ware Clarke, an American soldier killed in 1918, whose family originated in the area.

The brasses were unveiled in 1924 by Ambassador F. B. Kellog, and together with the generosity of the Americans who contributed to the fabric of an English country church, they bear witness to the sacrifice, the lasting friendship and fellow-feeling shared by our two nations, and continue a surprising connection, originated by Robert King, between the little Yorkshire town of Pickering and the capital of the United States of America.

American Connection
Photograph by Richard Hebblethwaite.

39. PORT MULGRAVE

The Hidden Harbour

Take the road to Hinderwell, 10 miles from Whitby on the A174 to Loftus. At the end of Hinderwell village take the right turn signposted to Port Mulgrave, past the Ship Inn on the right, to cottages on the left after ½ mile. A gate opposite gives access to a steep path down the cliff.

Many visitors to the Yorkshire coast are unaware of the tiny abandoned harbour which lies between Runswick Bay and Staithes. Like many 'lost villages' this little 'lost port' owes its demise to a change in the fortunes of industry. Port Mulgrave was built at the height of the iron mining boom in the 19th century, by Charles Palmer of Jarrow, where he owned several blast furnaces. He was also the founder of the Grinkle Park Mining Company and his idea was to control the process from start to finish by moving the ore from the mine to the port and from there shipping it to the blast furnaces. The ore was transported by narrow gauge railway from the mine and in order to get it down the steep cliffs the trucks were pulled by a stationary engine through a mile long tunnel to the harbour. The entrance to the tunnel, bricked up for safety, can still be seen.

At its peak the port handled some 3,000 tons of ore a week, but with the advent of cheaper ore from abroad the mine finally closed in the 1920s and Port Mulgrave was abandoned; a decaying reminder of a busy industrial past but well worth a visit for its historical interest and the magnificent views from the cliff tops.

The Hidden Harbour
Photograph by
Eileen Rennison

40. SALTERSGATE

The Turf Fire that never goes out

Saltersgate is about 8½ miles from Pickering on the A169 road to Whitby.

A short way beyond the Hole of Horcum on the Pickering to Whitby road is the Saltersgate Inn, where it is said that the peat fire in the bar has never been allowed to go out since about 1800. Legend has it that if the fire goes out then the ghost of an exciseman who was murdered there will return to haunt the place.

The inn was once a focus for smugglers carrying salt from Whitby along the route known as the Salt Road or the Old Fish Road. Salt was heavily taxed until 1825 and between 1798 and 1805 when the tax was most excessive there was a massive trade in the smuggling of salt and great efforts by Customs and Excise to put it down. This remote and solitary inn was an ideal store for smuggled salt and a centre for fishermen to salt their fish in readiness for transport inland.

It may be that originally the fire was kept burning simply to ensure that the stores of salt were kept dry. But was it also a means to prevent the discovery of a corpse hidden beneath it? In 1800 a lone exciseman was killed in a fight with a number of smugglers at the inn. Very soon afterwards a new fireplace was installed there, and his body, which was never found, is said to be buried under it.

Today's visitors to the Saltersgate Inn can gaze at that very fireplace with the fire still burning in the grate as they take their refreshment, and ask themselves — does it hide the bones of that old murder victim? Would his ghost return should the fire go out? No one is taking that risk. The tradition is kept and the fire continues to burn.

The Turf fire that never goes out
Photograph by Richard Hebblethwaite.

41. SCOTCH CORNER

Lonely Chapel of Remembrance

About 7½ miles from Helmsley on the A170 road to Thirsk, in the vicinity of the Hambleton Hotel, take a left turn along a narrow road to the Gliding Club and White Horse, to a point where two rough tracks unsuitable for vehicles branch off left. Continue on foot. Take the track sharp left, turning right after a short distance. Continue on a near straight line alongside, and then into High Wood, at the end of which take a smaller path right to the Chapel. Sensible walking shoes needed.

The Scotch Corner in question is not the one well known to motorists travelling north on the A1. This Scotch Corner lies on the Old Drove Road used in the 18th and 19th centuries by the drovers from Scotland and the North bringing their cattle and flocks down to markets in the South. Here the road branched off through Oldstead to the markets of the Plain of York, and hereabouts in a still earlier time the Battle of Byland was fought, when Edward II was put to flight by the Scots in 1322; hence the name of the spot.

The small chapel, arrived at unexpectedly in such a curious and isolated place, was once a farm building, until in the 1950s it was renovated and turned into a Chapel of Remembrance for those killed in battle and dedicated in particular to three former boys from Ampleforth College, the Roman Catholic Public school not far away, who were killed in World War II. The carvings outside of the Virgin and Child and an angel, and a Christ glimpsed through the door, are the work of John Bunting a local sculptor.

The chapel is not open to the public except at times when special services are held, but the carvings, the unusual site, the historic associations and the walk make it well worth a visit.

Lonely Chapel of Remembrance
Photograph by Eileen Rennison.

42. SHERIFF HUTTON

The Tomb of the Young Prince

From Malton take the A64 road to York turning right after about 4¼ miles to Welburn and Bulmer and Sheriff Hutton, a distance of a further 4½ miles. In the village the church lies to the left.

An ancient alabaster monument in a chapel of St. Helen and the Holy Cross at Sheriff Hutton is generally accepted to be that of Edward, Prince of Wales, the son of Richard the Third and his Queen, Anne Neville. Anne was the daughter of Warwick the Kingmaker, to whom Sheriff Hutton Castle, now a ruin, belonged. The young Prince is known to have died in Yorkshire at Middleham Castle in 1484 aged about eleven. His parents were in Nottingham at the time of his death, but returned immediately to Yorkshire for his burial. There is no actual record of that having taken place at Sheriff Hutton, or at any other place, and the effigy offers no inscription. However, the figure on the tomb is clearly that of a young boy of noble birth. He wears a long coat, known as a houppeland, and his head, bearing a coronet, rests on a pillow and griffins, or similar winged beasts. Altogether there seems little doubt that this must be the tomb of the young Prince Edward.

It has been damaged by age and damp but great efforts have been made over the years to preserve it, notably in 1950 by the founder of the Richard III Society and more recently in 1985 at the expense of that same society.

Tomb of Edward Prince of Wales, son of Richard III in Sheriff Hutton church Photograph by Eileen Rennison.

43. SINNINGTON

A Bridge over Nothing

3 miles out of Pickering on the A170 road to Helmsley take a right turn and continue less than 1 mile to Sinnington.

The village of Sinnington lies a little way off the main road between Pickering and Helmsley. It is a quiet and pretty place with all the features of the idealised English village: the stream crossed by a picturesque bridge: cottages with roses in the gardens: the village school set on the broad village green: a maypole with a fox atop as indication of the strong connection the village has with the ancient and well known Sinnington Hunt. Sadly when I visited the village the maypole was not in evidence. It seems that the wood had become rotten making it unsafe, and talk of a replacement in fibre-glass or plastic was causing some controversy and division amongst those for and against. But if the maypole was not on show, a much odder sight is to be seen on the village green. Some distance from the stream and spanning nothing but green grass is a tiny low arched packhorse style bridge. Perhaps the stream in the past ran on a different course or had a little branch. Whatever the reason for its presence there, this tiny, almost fairy-tale bridge left in isolation, going nowhere over nothing is an unusual and delightful feature of the village green.

Bridge over Nothing
Photograph by
Eileen Rennison.

44. STAITHES

The Traditional Bonnet

Staithes lies off to the right of the A174 road to Loftus about 10 miles from Whitby.

Staithes is a picturesque fishing village, once a centre for artists, attracted by the scenic effects of its red-roofed houses seemingly tumbling down its steep road to the sea, and the strong faces and proud bearing of the fisher-folk. Once a regular item of wear for the female population was the traditional bonnet. It can be seen in some of the photographs of Frank Meadow Sutcliffe, but it is not yet totally extinct and can still occasionally be seen today, worn by the older generation, or purchased as a sunhat by the tourist. It is made from one yard of cotton material cut into nine pieces to a pattern peculiar to the village, though with some similarity to the bonnets once worn by women everywhere. It is tied at the back with a bow and has a double crown and double pleated frill almost three inches wide at the front.

The reason for its origin and design is a matter of speculation but its purpose was certainly practical rather than decorative. The women of Staithes worked hard beside their menfolk and would carry the coiled fishing lines on their heads down to the boats. The bonnets then would serve as some protection to their hair; or perhaps, more simply they were to keep the hair free from the all-pervading fishy smell as the catch was dried and cured on the beach.

Whatever the reason for this particular headgear once being so common, the practicality and efficiency of the design has ensured the long survival of the bonnet as a curious relic from the past.

Staithes
Photograph by Eileen Rennison.

45. STONEGRAVE

Wills in Stone

Stonegrave is approximately 5½ miles from Helmsley on the B1257 road to Malton. The church lies off the road to the right.

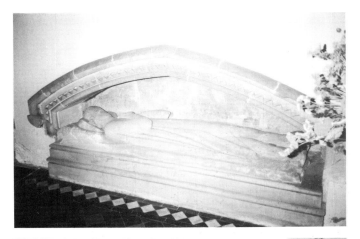

The church at Stonegrave, like St. Gregory's Minster, Kirkdale, is entitled to be called a Minster because it was once a kind of monastery to which a group of ordained monks was attached, serving a wide area around. The church stands in a quiet corner away from the road, overlooking the fields and surrounding countryside. There has been a church in this tranquil spot from the very earliest times and there are many features of interest as it has changed and developed over the ages.

It contains fragments of standing crosses and one almost complete cross, which were discovered in the 19th century but carved in the 9th and 10th centuries. The fragments are carved in a manner unique to Stonegrave and nowhere else in Ryedale. The larger cross is in a style traditional to Iona and Galloway in Scotland. There are also two medieval tombs with carved stone effigies, one of which is unusual, being of a civilian lying with his legs crossed, in the attitude more usually reserved for a knight.

But for the seeker of the unusual, two of the most interesting items are to be found in memorials from the 18th century which one could perhaps term Wills and Testaments in stone. The first, behind the font, sets out the details of a bequest intended as a continuing contribution to the maintenance of the fabric of the church, and apparently still doing so to this day. The second, by the door, is a clear statement of family members and heirs, presumably intended to prevent any disagreement over inheritance claims.

Wills in stone – Photographs by Eileen Rennison.

46. WESTERDALE

Bulmer's Stone

About 6½ miles from Pickering on the A170 to Helmsley, take a right turn to Hutton-le-Hole, approximately 2½ miles. Continue straight through the village to Westerdale, a further distance of about 10½ miles. The monument is in the garden of the first cottage on the right as one enters the village. It must be emphasised that it is in a private garden, but a quick view can be taken from the gate without intruding.

The stone pillar in a cottage garden in the village of Westerdale has a dramatic story of shipwreck and escape from death to tell. It is the work of one Thomas Bulmer, who retired to Westerdale and the cottage in question. With four boats carved at the base and almost every inch of the pillar itself covered with inscription, it seems intended both as a thanksgiving to God for his life after shipwreck and as a reminder to man of his mortality.

It is not easy to read but the date 1727 is followed by the words, *In this year it was my true intent to make here a lasting monument to show Thy mercies everywhere abound and save us when no mankind are to be found. Of this I have had large expieryance.* He then goes on to describe the circumstances in which he had the 'expieryance' of God's mercy during his journeys across the seas.

The inscription reads in part as follows:-

Bulmer's stone
Photographs by
Eileen Rennison.

Thomas Bulmer who lived here has often crossed the Main to many foreign shores, then Germany, Holland, France and Spain. Wrecked at length his frail bark the hopeful anchors cast is now unrigged and here lyeth moored fast. Tossed on rough seas on broken pieces of the ship until daybreak when they escaped all safe to land. Remember man thy sail on sea short it must be and then be turned to dust.

In the churchyard at Westerdale, against the rear wall of the church are two gravestones. Worn and covered in lichen they are even more difficult to decipher than the garden monument, but the one with skull and crossbones is that of Thomas Bulmer; the second of a boy aged only seventeen, also named Bulmer and dated like the monument 1727, leads one to wonder whether it could have been his son.

The stone pillar however, with its solemn and somewhat ambiguous words, has a special power of its own to inspire the imagination about Thomas Bulmer.

47. WHARRAM PERCY

The Lost Village

Take the B1248 road from Malton to Beverley for approximately 6 miles to Wharram-le-Street, ½ mile further turn right for Wharram Percy. At the car park leave car and walk for approximately 20 minutes to the deserted village.

Wharram Percy lies in a valley of the Wolds, south-east of Malton, and though signposts may point the way for motorists on the Malton to Beverley road, this is no ordinary village. It is one of the best preserved of the many recorded 'lost' villages of medieval days, deserted at different times and for varying reasons. Many villages were deserted as a result of the ravages of the Black Death. Wharram Percy was not one of these, but was a victim of the change from agriculture to sheep farming. The growth of the woollen cloth industry meant that landowners found it more profitable to give over their land to sheep, employing only a handful of men, rather than letting out the land to be cultivated in small parcels by the peasantry. As a result many villagers were dispossessed and had to seek a means of livelihood elsewhere.

By 1435 the village was reduced from thirty to sixteen houses and by the end of the century was finally deserted.

The church continued to be used by the people of Thixendale, a nearby village, until the nineteenth century, and despite the ravages of time, and the church's falling into ruin, an annual service is still held there.

Although no one lives there, and to the unimaginative eye its houses and roads are visible only as bumps and hollows, in a sense Wharram Percy is far from deserted. Over the past forty years at least, archaeologists have excavated on the site, learning a great deal from it, both of historical interest and in the refinement of archaeological techniques. The site is open all year round and many visitors and students make the journey past Wharram-le-Street down the narrow road to Wharram Percy car park, and walk along the medieval roadway to Wharram Percy itself, to stand in a village which is no more; no doubt to reflect on a community which worked and thrived, surely expecting to continue to do so for all time, yet had to uproot itself and disperse, and find a life elsewhere. The people are gone, the houses are gone and yet the village of Wharram Percy in a strange way still endures.

Wharram Percy
Photograph by Eileen Rennison.

48. WHITBY

The Hand of Glory

Take the A169 across the moors to Whitby 20 miles north of Pickering. The Whitby Museum is in Pannet Park.

The shrivelled Danby Hand of Glory can be seen, not in Danby but in the Whitby Museum in Pannet Park. As it lies in its glass case it looks a grisly but innocuous item; it is in fact an unusual and rare reminder of criminal history; a genuine human hand severed from the body of a criminal still hanging on the gibbet. Such a hand was once used by burglars as a charm to be carried with them on their criminal business. The hand — usually the right hand — which after being cut from a hanged man was then pickled and cured, was believed by them to make them invisible or in some other way protect them from arrest; a belief which must surely have been held despite evidence to the contrary! The name may well be explained as a corruption of the mandragora or mandrake plant whose roots were supposed to have similar magical powers, by way of its French corruption to Main de Glorie. As well as the power to make them invisible the hand was also believed by thieves to make sleeping people remain asleep and those who were awake remain awake; a highly desirable charm therefore for those who conducted their villainies at night.

To complete the charm the hard dried hand was to be

Hand of Glory
Photograph by
Eileen Rennison.

used as a candleholder, though the hand in the museum contains no candle. The candle itself was no ordinary candle, but must also have been made from such gruesome materials as the fat of a hanged man, with a wick made from the hair of a hanged man. As the candle was placed in the fingers of the hand and lit, ritual verses, which might vary from region to region, were chanted over it to call forth the magic powers. These could only be broken by extinguishing the flame, which in turn could only be achieved by pouring over it either milk or blood.

Until 1837 the penalty for burglary was death, and with such a risk involved it is perhaps not surprising that criminals clutched at any chance of reducing the possibility of capture, even to the extent of putting their faith in such bizarre superstitious charms. With the reduction of the penalty for burglary to imprisonment, the Hand of Glory gradually fell into disuse. The Danby Hand of Glory is thought to have been last used in 1820, and the last recorded use of such a charm was in 1831.

The Whalebone Monument at Whitby.

On the West Cliff, overlooking the ruined Abbey, at Whitby, stands a thirty foot high arch, formed from the jawbones of a hundred foot whale. This unusual monument commemorates Captain William Scoresby Snr. the leader of the prosperous nineteenth century Whitby Whaling Fleet and the man who perfected the crow's nest lookout. During his career Captain Scoresby killed five hundred and thirty-three whales and is commemorated as a successful man of his era who brought prosperity to the town. Today our thinking towards commercial whaling has changed as we strive to protect and preserve the whale. It may be that some will prefer to see the arch as a memorial to the whale.

Whalebone Arch
Photograph by Richard Hebblethwaite.